Craig Kielburger

Bryan Pezzi

Weigl

Published by Weigl Educational Publishers Limited
6325 10th Street S.E.
Calgary, Alberta T2H 2Z9
Website: www.weigl.com

Library and Archives Canada Cataloguing-in-Publication Data available upon request.
Fax (403) 233 7769 for the attention of the Publishing Records department.

ISBN 978-1-77071-597-4 (hard cover)
ISBN 978-1-77071-603-2 (soft cover)

Printed in the United States of America in North Mankato, Minnesota
1 2 3 4 5 6 7 8 9 0 14 13 12 11 10

072010
WEP230610

Editor: Aaron Carr   **Design:** Kenzie Browne

All of the Internet URLs given in the book were valid at the time of publication. However, due to the dynamic nature of the
Internet, some addresses may have changed, or sites may have ceased to exist since publication. While the author and publisher
regret any inconvenience this may cause readers, no responsibility for any such changes can be accepted by either the author or
the publisher.

We gratefully acknowledge the financial support of the Government of Canada through the Canada Book Fund for our
publishing activities.

Photo Credits
Free The Children: pages 3 top, 3 bottom, 5, 9, 10 top, 11 top, 11 bottom, 13, 15, 16; Getty Images: pages 1, 12, 17 top, 17
bottom, 19 top, 19 middle, 19 bottom, 20, 22 left, 22 right.

Every reasonable effort has been made to trace ownership and to obtain permission to reprint copyright material. The publishers
would be pleased to have any errors or omissions brought to their attention so that they may be corrected in subsequent printings.

CONTENTS

Who is Craig Kielburger?

Craig Kielburger is an **activist**, speaker, and writer. He travels the world working for children's **rights**. Kielburger started an organization called Free The Children at age 12. Free The Children helps children around the world stand up for their rights.

Kielburger often works with his brother, Marc. Together, Craig and Marc show children how they can make a difference.

The Kielburger brothers started Me to We in 2008. This company helps children travel the world to **volunteer** and learn leadership skills.

Growing Up

Craig Kielburger was born on December 17, 1982, in Thornhill, Ontario. His parents, Fred and Theresa, were both teachers. Kielburger's brother, Marc, is six years older than him.

Kielburger's life changed when he was 12 years old. One day, he picked up a newspaper to read the comics. He saw a story on the front page about a 12-year-old boy named Iqbal Masih. Masih was a **slave** in a carpet factory in Pakistan. After many years, Masih escaped. He told people what happened to him as a slave. Kielburger was shocked to learn children were living this way. He decided to help child slaves.

Ontario, Home of Craig Kielburger

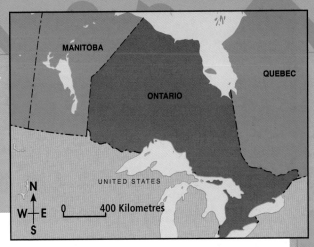

- Craig and Marc both work at the Free The Children main office in Toronto, Ontario.
- One out of every three Canadians lives in Ontario.
- The Ontario government awarded Kielburger the Ontario Medal for Good Citizenship. He won the award for his work in the community.
- The first Free The Children office was in Kielburger's family home.
- Me to We is based in Toronto.

Practice Makes Perfect

Kielburger talked to his classmates about child **labour**. In some parts of the world, children cannot go to school. They have to work many hours each day. Often, these children are treated poorly. They live and work in terrible conditions.

Kielburger and his classmates formed a group called Free The Children. The group made a display for a youth fair. The display taught people about child labour. Free The Children members also travelled to other schools to talk about children's rights.

9

Key Events

In 1995, a program about Free The Children aired on television. Later that year, Kielburger made a speech to 2,000 people at a labour **union** meeting. After his speech, the union gave $150,000 to Free The Children.

Kielburger wrote a book about his work in 1998. The book is called *Free the Children*. He has also written books about activism and **citizenship**.

In 1995, Kielburger went to Asia for seven weeks. There, he saw that children in other countries were often treated poorly. He returned from the trip eager to help children who had been forced to work as slaves.

Kielburger met the Dalai Lama in Sweden in 1998. The Dalai Lama is the **spiritual leader** of the Tibetan **Buddhist** religion. Kielburger said the meeting changed his life. Ten years later, Kielburger interviewed the Dalai Lama for a television show.

Influences

Iqbal Masih inspired Kielburger. Masih told people about child labour. He tried to help child slaves. At age 12, Masih was killed for speaking out about child labour. Kielburger never met him.

Kielburger's parents always supported his work. They taught him to be kind. Kielburger's parents planned his trip to Asia at age 12.

Marc was a role model to Craig. At age 13, Marc volunteered to help sick people in Jamaica. Sometimes, Craig helped Marc with his work.

13

Overcoming Obstacles

When Kielburger was young, he could not speak correctly. A **speech therapist** helped him with his speaking. Over time, Kielburger's speech improved. Later, Kielburger decided to try public speaking. He entered a speech contest and won a gold medal.

Kielburger faced many challenges after starting Free The Children. Being an activist at a young age was difficult. Kielburger was very busy. He had to balance his time between Free The Children and school.

Achievements and Successes

Free The Children has helped thousands of people. There are five Free The Children offices in North America. The organization has built more than 440 schools in 21 countries. It also provides clean water and health supplies to children in poor countries.

Free The Children tries to make sure people know when **goods** are made by child workers. The group hopes this will stop people from buying items made by children. Free The Children also works with families that are less fortunate. It helps them earn more money.

Kielburger has been on television shows such as *60 Minutes* and *CBC News*.

In 1999, Kielburger appeared on *The Oprah Winfrey Show*. After the show, Winfrey donated money to Free The Children. The money was used to build 34 schools.

In April 2006, Kielburger received the World's Children's Prize for the Rights of the Child. He was awarded the prize for "outstanding contributions to **defending** the rights of children."

What is an Activist?

An activist is a person who works to make the world a better place. Some activists help protect the environment. Others work to protect people's rights. Some activists help people who live in poor conditions. Activists take action in many ways. They write **petitions** and hold **rallies**. Activists also speak to reporters and **lobby** the government.

Activists Through History

Like Kielburger, these activists have achieved success.

Maude Barlow

Barlow leads The Council of Canadians. This group works to solve **social** problems in Canada. Barlow also works with other groups to help people around the world. She has written several books about social issues.

Stephen Lewis

Lewis is a Canadian **diplomat**. He works with other countries to solve problems around the world. In Africa, many people suffer from war, poor living conditions, and illness. Lewis raises money and awareness of these issues.

Naomi Klein

Klein is a Canadian **journalist**. She wrote a book called *No Logo*. It is about companies that do not pay their workers fairly. Most often, these workers live in poor countries.

Timeline

1982	Craig Kielburger is born on December 17 in Ontario.
1989	Marc takes Craig to hear a speech about saving the environment.
1995	Kielburger reads about Iqbal Masih in the newspaper. He starts Free The Children. Later, Kielburger travels to Asia for seven weeks.

1998	Kielburger's book, *Free the Children*, is released. The same year, he meets the Dalai Lama in Sweden.
1999	Kielburger appears on *The Oprah Winfrey Show*.
2001	Kielburger and Marc publish *Take Action: A Guide to Active Citizenship*.
2006	Kielburger is awarded the World's Children's Prize for the Rights of the Child.
2008	Kielburger interviews the Dalai Lama for a television show.

Write a Biography

A person's life story can be the subject of a book. This kind of book is called a biography. Biographies describe the lives of people who have had great success or done important things to help others. These people may be alive today, or they may have lived many years ago.

Try writing your own biography. First, decide who you want to write about. You can choose an activist, such as Craig Kielburger, or any other person you find interesting.

Then, find out if your library has any books about this person. Write down the key events in this person's life.

- What was this person's childhood like?
- What has he or she accomplished?
- What are his or her goals?
- What makes this person special or unusual?

Answer the questions in your notebook. Your answers will help you write a biography.

Find Out More

To learn more about Craig Kielburger, visit these websites.

Learn about Free The Children at this site.
www.freethechildren.com

Go to this site, and type "Craig Kielburger" into the Hero Search.
www.myhero.com/go/search

This site has more information about Kielburger.
www.cbc.ca/news/
background/kielburger

Visit this site to learn more about Me to We.
www.metowe.com

Glossary

activist: a person who works for a cause

Buddhist: a person who follows the teachings of Buddha

citizenship: the rights and responsibilities of people who belong to a country

defending: protecting from harm

diplomat: a person whose job is to represent his or her country

goods: items that can be sold

journalist: a person who reports the news

labour: physically challenging work

lobby: try to get a person or organization to act a certain way

petitions: documents that people sign to show support for a cause

rallies: gatherings of people to raise support for a cause

rights: equal treatment of all people

slave: a person who is kept as property and forced to work

social: anything related to groups of people living together

speech therapist: a person that helps people improve their speech

spiritual leader: a leader of a religious group

union: a group of workers who join together to fight for their rights

volunteer: working for no pay

Index